Pebble™ Plus

Healthy Eating with MyPyramid

The Grain Group

by Mari C. Schuh

Consulting Editor: Gail Saunders-Smith, PhD

Consultant: Barbara J. Rolls, PhD
Guthrie Chair in Nutrition
The Pennsylvania State University
University Park, Pennsylvania

Capstone press
Mankato, Minnesota

Pebble Plus is published by Capstone Press,
151 Good Counsel Drive, P.O. Box 669, Mankato, Minnesota 56002.
www.capstonepress.com

1 2 3 4 5 6 11 10 09 08 07 06

Library of Congress Cataloging-in-Publication Data
Schuh, Mari C., 1975–
    The grain group / by Mari C. Schuh.
    p. cm.—(Pebble Plus. Healthy eating with MyPyramid)
    Summary: "Simple text and photographs present the grain group, the foods in the group, and examples of
healthy eating choices"—Provided by publisher.
    Includes bibliographical references and index.
    ISBN-13: 978-0-7368-5371-2 (hardcover)
    ISBN-10: 0-7368-5371-5 (hardcover)
    1. Cereals as food—Juvenile literature. 2. Grain—Juvenile literature. 3. Nutrition—Juvenile literature.
I. Title. II. Series.
TX393.S38 2006
641.3'31—dc22
          2005023706

Credits
Jennifer Bergstrom, designer; Kelly Garvin, photo researcher; Stacy Foster and Michelle Biedscheid,
    photo shoot coordinators

Photo Credits
BananaStock Ltd., 1
Capstone Press/Karon Dubke, cover, 3, 5, 9, 11, 13, 14–15, 17, 18–19, 21, 22 (all)
Corbis/Peter Beck, 6–7
U.S. Department of Agriculture, 10 (inset), 11 (computer screen)

The author dedicates this book to her parents, Mona and Dan Schuh of Fairmont, Minnesota.

**Information in this book supports the U.S. Department of Agriculture's MyPyramid for Kids
food guidance system found at http://www.MyPyramid.gov/kids. Food amounts listed in this
book are based on an 1,800-calorie food plan.**

**The U.S. Department of Agriculture (USDA) does not endorse any products, services,
or organizations.**

Note to Parents and Teachers

The Healthy Eating with MyPyramid set supports national science standards related to
nutrition and physical health. This book describes and illustrates the grain group. The
images support early readers in understanding the text. The repetition of words and
phrases helps early readers learn new words. This book also introduces early readers
to subject-specific vocabulary words, which are defined in the Glossary section. Early
readers may need assistance to read some words and to use the Table of Contents,
Glossary, Read More, Internet Sites, and Index sections of the book.

Table of Contents

Grains

Grains give you energy.
What grains have you
eaten today?

Do you know that grains

are parts of plants?

Most grains grow in fields.

Oats, corn, wheat,

and rice are grains.

Try to eat foods that

are made from whole grains.

Whole grains are

full of nutrients.

MyPyramid for Kids

MyPyramid teaches you
the foods and amounts
that are right for you.
The grain group is
a part of MyPyramid.

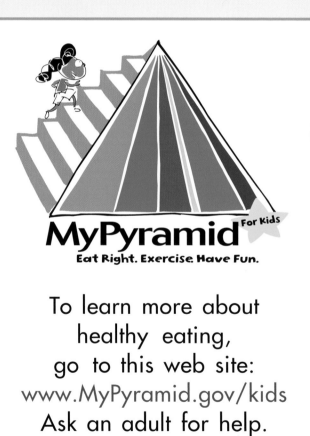

To learn more about
healthy eating,
go to this web site:
www.MyPyramid.gov/kids
Ask an adult for help.

Nibble, nibble, nibble.
Try to eat 6 ounces
of grains a day.

13

Enjoying Grains

Chewy, yummy,

and good for you.

Eat a sandwich for lunch.

Choose whole-grain bread.

Pop, pop, pop!

Make popcorn

in the microwave.

Share it with your friends.

The noodles in your soup
are made from grain.
Slurp!

Grains are a part
of a healthy meal.
What are your
favorite grains?

How Much to Eat

Many kids need to eat 6 ounces of grains every day. To get 6 ounces, pick six of your favorite grains below.

Pick six grains to eat today!

½ cup cooked pasta

5 whole-wheat crackers

2 small pancakes

½ cup cooked rice

½ cup cooked spaghetti

3 cups low-fat popcorn

1 cup of cereal

1 slice of bread

Glossary

MyPyramid—a food plan that helps kids make healthy food choices and reminds kids to be active; MyPyramid was created by the U.S. Department of Agriculture.

nutrient—something that people need to eat to stay healthy and strong; vitamins and minerals are nutrients.

whole grain—a food that has all three parts of a grain seed; whole grains have lots of vitamins, minerals, and fiber that is good for your body; at least half of your grains should be whole grains.

Read More

Nelson, Robin. *Grains.* First Step Nonfiction. Minneapolis: Lerner, 2003.

Rondeau, Amanda. *Grains Are Good.* What Should I Eat? Edina, Minn.: Abdo, 2003.

Thomas, Ann. *Grains.* Food. Philadelphia: Chelsea Clubhouse, 2003.

Index

Word Count: 130
Grade: 1
Early-Intervention Level: 15

Internet Sites

FactHound offers a safe, fun way to find Internet sites related to this book. All of the sites on FactHound have been researched by our staff.

Here's how:

1. Visit *www.facthound.com*

2. Type in this special code **0736853715** for age-appropriate sites. Or enter a search word related to this book for a more general search.

3. Click on the **Fetch It** button.

FactHound will fetch the best sites for you!